HAPPY CUSTOMERS FASTER CASH

Ireland chapters

A guide to effective communication in financial Customer Relationship Management

Declan Flood

Marcel Wiedenbrugge - Cliff Wynn

Cover design: Patrick van der Doef

Preface Ireland edition

I am honoured to be asked to participate in this book, I have known Marcel and Cliff for many years and I know they are as committed as I am to promote best practice in Credit Management on an International stage, while maintaining local understanding. In my contribution, I hope to give you an insight into Ireland, doing business in Ireland and any other information I think you would find useful. - Enjoy

Declan Flood, Ireland

CONTENTS

CHAPTER 1: CREDIT MANAGEMENT IN IRELAND

1.1 Credit Management in Ireland

The first thing anyone doing business in Ireland needs to know is that there are two distinct and completely different jurisdictions on the Island. The six counties in the North-East of the island is known as Northern Ireland, it is part of the United Kingdom, the currency they use is Sterling and measure their distances in miles. The rest of the country is known as the Republic of Ireland, it is a separate country that uses Euro as their currency and distances are measured in Kilometres.

There are different laws and business practices and a different attitude to credit in both jurisdictions, and in the paragraphs that follow, I will give you an insight into the similarities and the differences, to help you get the most out of doing business in Ireland.

The Irish are renowned for their easy going attitude, and while this can be a major asset when it comes to holidays and enjoying life, this same attitude can also extend to the operation of trade credit and particularly for The Republic of Ireland so, an active credit control system is required to ensure prompt payment.

Credit Policies

Amazingly most companies in Ireland do not have a written credit policy that is communicated and enforced across the business. Of course, this is something I would encourage every business to do, no matter their size. They should set out the rules around granting credit for the benefit of customers and other sections of the business alike. I have written previously that after the Vision & Mission Statement, the credit policy is the most important document in any business. The vision and mission statements set out where the business wants to go and the Credit Policy sets out how it is going to get there.

Payment Terms

Payment terms range from Pro-Forma invoice (i.e. Payment in advance) to 120 days credit. Most stated terms are 30 days and that would normally be interpreted to mean that payment is due at the end of the month following invoice. Some industries like Hospitality and Construction, the standard terms are 60 days i.e. payment is due at the end of the second month after invoice. Government Departments are supposed to pay on 15 days, and all payments from Government agencies are electronic since 15th September 2014. According to the latest European Directive on Late Payments, Government Departments are obliged to pay late payment interest if payment is not made as agreed. Some will calculate the interest themselves and include it with the payment; others need a separate invoice for interest. When it comes to calculating interest, Northern Ireland uses the Bank of England as their base and in the Republic they use the European Central Bank rates.

Payment Methods

Traditionally cheques have been the preferred method of payment in Ireland. Currently there is a big shift to bank transfers and as part of the European Payment system SEPA, most businesses preferred payment methods are Bank transfer for larger amounts and credit card for small amounts. PayPal is also widely used in Ireland. While cheques are still accepted by most private organisations, current bank charges and fees are designed in such a way to make this form of payment unattractive, nevertheless cheques are still the preferred method of payment in a number of sectors, particularly in traditional areas like farming and construction

The 19thSeptember 2014 was E-day in Ireland and is the date from which Government Departments, Local Authorities and State Agencies no longer use cheques in their dealings with businesses.

Credit Information Providers & Credit Management Services

Some people think that Credit Management in Ireland can be difficult. This can be the case with some and not with others. Ireland has two main types of businesses, firstly most of the major Multinationals are headquartered in Ireland and secondly there is a huge SME sector which accounts for most of the Companies and most of the employment.

When it comes to payment, you will find that as long as your invoices are correct and in total agreement with the purchase order, payment will be processed promptly, if you have problems with your own invoicing, you will have to resolve that issue first before you can expect to receive any payment. There are two ways of dealing with an incorrect invoice: some companies will pay the amount they think they should pay and raise a credit request for the balance, others will not make any payment until a correct invoice is received and processed. While there are exceptions, businesses in Northern Ireland are more likely to withhold the full payment, whereas businesses in the Republic will generally pay the reduced amount.

In the SME sector, you should always send out an invoice with clear credit terms stating the exact day that payment is due. Depending on the value and importance of that invoice to you a telephone or email reminder before the due date or immediately afterwards is a good idea.

The Irish attitude to credit is that if the Creditor isn't pursuing payment actively, they obviously don't want the money, so they are put to the bottom of the priority list.

Getting information on Irish registered companies is easy. There are two main sources of information. Firstly you can get on to the Companies Office Directly www.cro.ie . By law companies have to file their accounts on an annual basis, each Company is given an ARD (Annual Return Date) that they must have their accounts filed by. This is typically nine months after the Financial Year End. On the website you can search or purchase information. You can search the company name, status, ARD, Registered number, the date the last accounts were filed etc. for free. If you want to download any of the documents, there is a nominal fee for each one of around €3.50.

There is an excellent service called Search4less (www.search4less.ie) For a low annual subscription, you get unlimited access to all the company information and documents for a full year. This database is also easily searchable and you can find details of People, Business Names, Judgments, Revenue Default, Bankruptcy as well as the regular Company information. This service also gives you unlimited documents from the Companies Office for The Republic and a small charge for Northern Ireland Documents.

All the major Information providers operate in the Irish market such as Dun & Bradstreet (D&B), Experian, CreditSafe, and company check. Some get payment performance data to enhance the numbers received from the Companies Office that gives a more up to date view on how the business is performing.

Most of the major information providers will give you a credit rating and a credit limit for the buyer, it is my belief that one size cannot fit all, so an intelligent application of the information received would be a good idea. Depending on the formula each agency uses you can see divergent results, my advice here is to check out the one that suits your business best.

There are also a number of local information providers e.g. Vision-Net, Stubbs Gazette and Solo Check.

Public Holidays
(NI = Northern Ireland, ROI = Republic of Ireland)

New Year's Day - 1st January every year (ROI/NI) If the 1st falls on a Saturday or Sunday, the Monday becomes the Bank Holiday (ROI/NI)

St Patricks Day - 17th March every year . If the 17th falls on a Saturday or Sunday, the Monday becomes the Bank Holiday (ROI/NI)

Good Friday – is a Bank Holiday in NI, In ROI it is a bank holiday but not a public holiday. Some businesses work and some don't. There is no real consistency so you should check with your customers on this one.

Easter Monday (ROI/NI)

May Day Bank Holiday is always on the first Monday in May (ROI/NI)

Spring Bank Holiday is on the last Monday in May (NI)

June Bank Holiday is on the first Monday in June (ROI)

The Twelfth - July 12th – Is a Public Holiday (NI) If the 12th falls on a Saturday or Sunday, the Monday becomes the Bank Holiday (NI)

August Bank Holiday is on the first Monday in August in ROI and the last Monday in August in NI

October Bank Holiday is always on the last Monday in October (ROI)

Christmas Day – 25th December (ROI/NI) If the 25th falls on a Saturday or Sunday, the Monday becomes the Bank Holiday (ROI/NI)

St Stephens Day – 26th December (ROI) If the 26th falls on a Saturday or Sunday, the Monday/ Tuesday becomes the Bank Holiday (ROI)

Boxing Day – 26th December (NI) If the 17th falls on a Saturday or Sunday, the Monday/ Tuesday becomes the Bank Holiday (NI)

While the holiday dates above are the official dates, in reality very few people work on Christmas Eve and most will return to work on the first working day of January. Some industries like food and retail will open as usual on the days between Christmas and the New Year.

Debt Collection

There are a number of Collection agencies operating in Ireland. It is still an unregulated activity, so care should be taken in choosing an agency that will work with you. The main players are: Intrum Justitia, AR Solutions, Stubbs Gazette, LCMS and Everyday Collections. Normally agencies work on a commission basis on the amount collected, there is no strict code so, all details e.g. who the payments are made out to, should be agreed in advance. There are different rates charged based on the values and age of the debt, typically rates range from 15% to 25%.

There is a formal debt collection process through the courts. There are three main courts:

District Court can hear cases up to €15,000
Circuit Court can hear cases up to €75,000
High Court has no Limit
Commercial Court hears cases over €1 million

Like most countries, legal proceedings can be costly and time consuming. You should get legal advice before proceeding down this route. You should also make sure that the cost of collecting what you are owed does not exceed the amount collectable.

There are a number of enforcement options that should be explored to make sure there are sufficient assets to meet your debt.

The simple rule when it comes to legal action:

- Do I have all the information?
- Do they have the resources to make the payment?

If the answer is yes then proceed, if not, don't!

The main Irish Legal firms in the Debt Collection area are:

AB Wolfe   : www.abwolfe.ie
Croskerrys   : www.croskerrys.com
Ivor Fitzpatick & Co   : www.ivorfitzpatrick.ie
Hugh J Ward   : www.hughjwardsolicitors.ie
Lavelle Solicitors   : www.lavellesolicitors.ie
Tracey Solicitors   : www.traceysolicitors.ie

Perception of Credit Management

In most companies, Credit Management is still perceived as primarily a debt collection function and while collections is an important element, it is only one part of the overall process which ideally should begin with identifying leads, opening new accounts through to putting the money in the bank.

In some businesses, the credit controller is responsible for opening new accounts, the management of the administration function, invoicing, credit notes and monthly statements, the creation of reports and the timely collection of all money outstanding. I recommend looking at your business model and to see if it would benefit from expanding the credit management responsibilities to include the cycle from "prospecting to cash".

New Personal Insolvency Legislation

In 2012 new Personal Insolvency legislation was enacted to give options to individuals who are experiencing financial difficulties. They range from Bankruptcy, that takes three years to be discharged, to Debt Relief Notice (DRN) for individuals with lower amounts of debt (i.e. Less that €20k) for full details see www.isi.gov.ie

Credit Insurance

Credit Insurance is used only by a small percentage of businesses in Ireland. There have been a number of products launched that are specifically for the SME. The question is "Do you have or should you get Credit Insurance?" My advice here is that it depends on the profile of your ledger.

If you have a large number of small balances, where your risk is split and any one loss will not have a substantial impact on your business, then I would suggest that credit insurance is not that important to you.

If you have a limited number of customers with very high balances the question is: if one of your key customers went out of business, would it have a major impact on yours? If so, then I would recommend looking at credit insurance as a method of mitigating your exposure. It is not a substitute for excellent credit management, it is a way of reducing your own losses over a given period of time.

There are three main players in Ireland:

Atradius   : www.atradius.ie

Coface   : www.cofaceuk.com/Ireland

Euler Hermes   : www.eulerhermes.co.uk

There are also a number of brokers, who will work with you to make sure you get the cover you need at a reasonable cost. One factor you have to take into account when choosing a credit insurer is: how much admin work and reporting is involved? This can be a hidden factor, and should be considered.

Credit Management Training & Advice

Irish Credit Management Training have been providing excellent training in all aspects of credit in Ireland for over twelve years. They cover trade and consumer credit and the full scope from Credit Risk Assessment to Collections. They can be contacted on www.icmt.ie.

1.2 Useful links about credit management, doing business and business culture in Ireland

Country Risk Guides

Coface: www.coface.com/Economic-Studies-and-Country-Risks

A.M. Best: www3.ambest.com/ratings/cr/reports/Ireland.pdf

Euler Hermes:

www.eulerhermes.com/economic-research/Pages/Interactive-country-risk-map.aspx

Credit Information (B2B) & Credit Bureaus

Irish Credit Bureau: www.icb.ie

The objectives of the ICB, which have the support of regulatory authorities and consumer groups, are as follows:

- To assist the lowering of the cost of credit
- To enable faster decisions in providing credit
- To aid the avoidance of over indebtedness
- To assist with fraud prevention

StubbsGazette: www.stubbsgazette.ie

StubbsGazette Credit Bureau is an extensive credit checking facility on businesses and individuals in Ireland. You can access CRO documents, disqualified directors, bankruptcies, and data exclusive to Stubbs

Dun &Bradstreet: www.dnb.ie

International Information Providers

Experian: www.experian.ie

International Information Providers

Company Watch: www.companywatch.co.uk

All the financial information, well laid out for all companies in Ireland, Northern Ireland and the UK for a small monthly fee.

CreditSafe: www.creditsafe.ie

National and International Company Reports

VisionNet: www.vision-net.ie

Irish Information Providers and producers of the business barometer

Credit Insurance

www.icisa.org

ICISA is the International Credit Insurance Surety Association. Under "Publication" you can download the Yearbook 2014 2015, which provides a global overview of credit insurance companies in which countries they are active. The main credit insurance companies active in the Ireland are:

Atradius: www.atradius.ie

Euler Hermes: www.eulerhermes.co.uk

AON: www.aon.com/ireland/risk-services/trade-credit.jsp

Cimco Ireland: www.cimco.ie

Trade Credit Brokers: www.tcbrokers.com

All of these companies offer a wide range of specialized products including debt collection services to enable companies to conduct business more safely both in the U.S. and overseas. One or more credit insurance companies may also specialize in specific business sectors.

Credit Management Associations

IICM. Irish Institute of Credit Management

www.iicm.ie

ICTF. The association of International Credit and Trade Finance professionals

www.ictfworld.org

FCIB. International Association of Executives in Finance, Credit and International Business.

www.fcibglobal.com

FECMA. Federation of European Credit Management Associations
www.fecma.eu

FENCA. Federation of European National Collection Agencies
www.fenca.org

Credit Management Training

Irish Credit Management Training: www.icmt.ie

Credit Management Education & Training

The Credit Coach: www.declanflood.ie

Credit Management Training and Consultancy

Debt Collection & Debt Recovery

The **Atradius Debt Collection Handbook** (8th edition): www.atradiuscollections.com/global

The Atradius Debt Collection Handbook can be downloaded from this website. It contains information on debt collection procedures, rules and regulations in 40 countries, including Ireland.

Euler Hermes Economic research "International debt collection – The Good, The Bad and the Ugly", in which debt collection in 44 countries is (briefly) analyzed including Ireland.

www.eulerhermes.com/mediacenter/Lists/mediacenter-documents/Economic-Outlook-International-Debt-Collection-1213-dec14.pdf

Debt Collection Agencies in Ireland

AR Solutions: www.arsolutions.ie

Atradius Collections: www.atradiuscollections.com/global

Cabot Financial (Ireland) Ltd: www.cabotfinancial.ie

Everyday Group: www.everydaygroup.ie

Intrum Justitia: www.intrum.com/ie

LCMS: www.lcms.ie

Stubbs Gazette: www.stubcollections.com

Doing business in Ireland – country guides

Doing Business 2016 guide published by the World Bank. A complete source of information comparing business regulations for domestic firms in 189 economies.
www.doingbusiness.org

The Worldbank database: http://data.worldbank.org/country/ireland?display=map

Supporting SMEs: www.localenterprise.ie/smeonlinetool/businessdetails.aspx

This is an online guide to help Irish start-ups and small businesses to navigate the range of government supports and which ones may apply to you. Though focused at Irish companies, the information provided can be useful for (small) foreign companies active in Ireland as well.

European Late Payment Directive

The European Late Payment Directive aims to fight late payment in the European Union. http://ec.europa.eu/enterprise/policies/single-market-goods/fighting-late-payments/index_en.htm

Irish culture

Various websites about business culture, communication and business ethics in Ireland:

www.everyculture.com/Ge-It/Ireland.html

http://www.executiveplanet.com/ireland-2/

http://guide.culturecrossing.net/basics_business_student.php?id=100

www.internations.org

Legal system in Ireland

http://global.practicallaw.com/8-502-0560

Detailed information on debt recovery, insolvency procedures and the legal system in Ireland

Payment behaviour

In Ireland, many (public) sources are available to gain more insight into the payment behavior of Irish companies. Traditionally credit insurance companies have a reasonably good up to date insight into payment behaviour of companies in most economies, including Ireland. Especially Atradius and Coface sometimes publish corporate payment survey results. Occasionally D&B also publishes corporate payment studies.

SME Credit Demand Survey – April – September 2014

www.finance.gov.ie/news-centre/press-releases/sme-credit-demand-survey-april-september-2014

Central Bank of Ireland. Search under "publications" for "SME Market Report".

www.centralbank.ie/publications/Pages/default.aspx

European Payment Report
A survey about payment behaviour and payment risks in Europe conducted in 29 countries (B2B and B2C).
www.intrum.com/press-and-publications/european-payment-report

Atradius Payment Barometer Ireland

https://group.atradius.com/reports-and-advice/payment-practices-barometer-ireland-2015.html

Payment systems and methods

www.thepaypers.com/ecommerce-facts-and-figures/uk/6

The Paypers insights in payments website. This page provides an overview of preferred ecommerce facts & figures, payment methods, online fraud prevention, payment service providers, (payment) news and reports about the United Kingdom, not specifically Ireland.

Various Financial Institutions

Central Bank of Ireland: www.centralbank.ie

The high level goals of the Central Bank of Ireland are summarised as follows:

- Eurosystem effectiveness and price stability
- Stability of the financial system
- Proper and effective regulation of financial institutions and markets
- Resolution of financial difficulties in credit institutions
- Independent economic advice and high quality financial statistics
- Efficient and effective payment and settlement systems and currency services
- Operational efficiency and cost effectiveness

CHAPTER 2: COMMUNICATION WITH THE CUSTOMER

2.1 Irish business culture and communication

Irish People in General

Irish people are renowned for their friendliness, and as such will be less formal than other European countries. It is customary to refer to a person by their first name, in all conversations and correspondence.

Because credit tends to be a people business it is always advisable to get the name of the person who looks after the payment of your account, with ongoing contact it is important you build and maintain a good working relationship with them, I don't know if it is exclusively Irish or if it is universal, people tend to pay the people they like.

Irish Culture

There is a stereotypical view of Ireland and the Irish, where Ireland is seen as a backward traditional farming country where the natives fight and drink.

The reality of modern Ireland is far removed from this picture. Ireland has become a multicultural society, young, well educated and vibrant. At the time of writing, 2015, Ireland is well positioned to emerge from the downturn, with all economic indicators pointing to a growing economy. Employment levels are heading for an all-time high and the economy is boosted by a large number of high tech companies, in both IT and Pharmaceuticals.

Most students go on to third level education providing an excellent resource to build on. Ireland are committed to the European Union and for its size is an influential member of the union. While agriculture and food production are still very important pillars of our economy, it is delivered through driving best practices that ensure that Irish food products are rightly considered premium quality.

Of course our traditional industries have been streamlined and modernised, Jameson Irish Whiskey is a premium brand worldwide, not to mention our most famous export – Guinness. Of course, like them or not; Irish Airline – Ryanair, has become the largest airline in Europe when measured by the number of passengers carried.

In the past there have been lapses in Regulation and Compliance issues, these are now being addressed which will enhance Irelands reputation as a country others want to do business with. We are the only country in the EU that exports more than we consume, and these valuable exports continue to be the source of ongoing wealth. The Government are committed to openness and transparency in all business dealings and this will bode well for future expansion.

The Irish now have a reputation of working hard and playing hard, this is as true today as ever before. It is running on technology but still values the interpersonal interactions at every possible opportunity. It is not uncommon for your Irish business partner to become your friend that is how we do business.

Effective Communication in Credit Management

The preferred method of communication in most medium and large companies is email, and in smaller companies the telephone works best. Letters work better in Northern Ireland than they do in the South.

You are advised to have clear terms, agreed in advance and make sure you follow up actively. Waiting for the money to come in will send out the message that getting paid is not important to you, and will result in delays. Train your staff and make sure they actively pursue all outstanding balances as quickly as possible, and if possible before the due date, to ensure payments are made in full and on time.

As this publication is geared for the SME sector there are a number of do's and don'ts to observe, this list is not exhaustive and is designed to give you a simple checklist to implement to improve the cash flow and profitability of your business

Do's:

- Invoice daily if possible and weekly at worst, to make sure your invoices are processed in a timely manner
- Make sure your invoices are correct in every detail, purchase order numbers, quantities, pricing and the proper legal entity.
- Call early to arrange payment.
- Send out statements (to customers who want them) on the first working day of every month.
- Have a dedicated person who is responsible for cash collection (not the owner, unless a one man band)
- Set cash collection targets monthly.
- Have very clear credit terms
- Develop a clear process to deal with unpaid accounts in a systematic way

Don'ts

- Never fight with your customers (particularly about money)
- Give credit without performing some form of credit check on potential customers.
- Run out of money

A business can lose money many times, they can only run out of money once. Still today, businesses fail because they simply run out of cash. Take the advice in this book to make sure your business goes from strength to strength by ensuring you get paid for everything you do.

12 excuses for late payment and how to deal with them

Below we have listed 12 excuses. We will discuss each excuse in detail, provide an example and show you how to deal effectively with each excuse.

1. *We never received the invoice*
2. *We always pay our invoices after 60 days*
3. *I just paid the invoice*
4. *I really don't understand it. I paid a few days ago*
5. *The payment has not been authorized, because the person responsible for approving invoices (departmental manager or general manager) is not available/out of the office.*
6. *We never received the goods*
7. *My customer has not paid me yet*
8. *The invoice was incorrect and I am still waiting for a credit note*
9. *The order was cancelled*
10. *My customer went bankrupt.*
11. *The financial paperwork is at my accountant's office.*
12. *The managing director is on vacation and he needs to approve the payment.*

EXCUSE #1

Customer: '*We never received the invoice.*'

Supplier: '*If I send you a copy by email today, can you organise payment to us before Friday?* [If there is a reason to doubt the customer's statement, you can indirectly indicate that not receiving an invoice is a very rare event, so the customer will have to think of another excuse in the future]

Explanation

This excuse is frequently used and may be true. Although delivery times may vary from country to country and guarantees of delivery are not provided, most post ultimately arrives at its destination. If it is a particularly high value or important invoice you may want check your local postal service for estimated delivery times, traceability and possibly use a guaranteed and signed for delivery service.

A customer who claims that he did not receive the invoice, often, but not always, means that the customer has lost the invoice or incorrectly 'filed' the invoice (i.e. the invoice lies somewhere in the proverbial pile of documents to be processed, in other words the administration is probably a mess). If you notice that the same customer frequently uses this excuse, it is a good idea to monitor the customer more closely. So for future deliveries you could contact the customer a few days after the delivery took place to check if the customer has received the invoice. If the customer wants to know the reason for your call, you can tell him that it is important to you that invoices are produced promptly and arrive addressed to the correct person. After all, it is important for both the customer and the supplier that invoices are correct and sent in a timely manner. By dealing with the situation in this way, you will leave a professional impression, improve customer experience and, over time, it may lead to improved payment behaviour by your customer.

EXCUSE #2

Customer: '*We always pay our invoices after 60 days.*'

Supplier: '*I hear what you are saying, but, our terms and conditions clearly state that your payment terms are 30 days net and you know that. I would like to talk to you about how we can prevent these payment issues in the future?*' Alternative: '*I hear what you are saying, but how would you feel if I bought goods from you on 30 days net, but then paid after 60 days?*' [wait for their response and then dig deeper into the topic]

Explanation

Customers can sometimes be very creative by inventing their own payment terms. The explanation for such behaviour is not always clear, but often these types of customers think that they are so important to a supplier that they will be happy to do business with them no matter what payment terms they might invent. In such cases it can be very difficult to get the customer back in line again. On the one hand it would not be fair to allow one or a few customers to have different, more favourable terms, but on the other hand you may not want to offend the customer and possibly lose their business. It takes patience and a clear strategy, to know what to do with such customers. Therefore you need to understand the future commercial importance of such customers and discuss how to proceed with the sales department. Changing payment behaviour is often a time consuming process. Being consistent and reminding the customer of the terms in a friendly way will maintain the relationship and may improve payment behaviour. However, if this doesn't work you need to decide, in conjunction with sales, whether to continue the customer relationship or gradually say goodbye.

EXCUSE #3

Customer: '*I just paid the invoice*'

Jenkins: '*That's good news. Did you pay the invoice electronically?*' [wait for a reply] '*When exactly did you pay the invoice (or outstanding amount)?*' [wait for a reply]. Alternative: '*How much did you pay and to which bank account?*' [wait for a reply]? '*If you paid yesterday, it should be visible on our statement tomorrow at the latest. I will check then, thanks for your time.*'

Explanation

This reply is probably the one you will hear the most and it is very easy for the customer to use. However, you can easily check if the customer is telling you the truth or not. A payment processed by the customer cannot be reversed, unless the bank refuses to execute the transaction due to lack of funds or insufficient credit. During the conversation, you don't need to tell the customer you will contact him again if you do not receive the payment within one or two days. You will contact the customer anyway if the payment doesn't show up on your bank statement. When a customer uses this excuse often it may indicate that you are dealing with an undisciplined or unorganised customer. It may also mean that they are in a poor financial position, so when in doubt you better check their creditworthiness. With these types of customers it is important to stay in close control and send reminders shortly after the due date. A proactive, but customer-friendly, reminder strategy may work as well. Credit management software and automated collections strategies can obviously help a lot to improve payment behaviour.

HINT

If you ask the customer to send a copy or print screen of the electronic payment, be aware that the payment has actually been processed, so the customer cannot delete the payment instruction afterwards. However, a payment that has been instructed does not necessarily mean that the payment is processed. If the credit limit or overdraft facility of your customer with his bank has been exceeded, the bank may decide not to execute the payment instruction. One of the fastest and most reliable ways of getting paid is by phone payment (telephone banking), where your bank confirms receipt of the payment via email or by telephone.

EXCUSE #4

Customer: *'I really don't understand it. I paid a few days ago.'*

Jenkins: *'A couple of days ago I talked to you and you told me that you paid the outstanding invoice/invoices. What has happened, did the bank not process your payment?'* [wait for a reply] *'Well, if you could arrange a payment today we can clear the account.'* [optional] *'Could you telephone me when you have processed the payment and I can check our account to confirm receipt of the payment? Is that OK with you?'* [wait for a reply] *'Great, I look forward to receiving the payment. I hope you have a good day and I am pleased we could resolve this issue.'*

Explanation

If you have to call the customer because he did not meet his commitment to pay you on a specific date, it usually means one of two things:

The customer simply did not make the payment

The bank has not approved the payment instruction due to a negative balance or other financial problems with the customer.

The first case suggests that you are dealing with a lazy or unreliable customer. The second case may mean that your customer has liquidity or cash flow problems, so you also need to check the creditworthiness of the customer. If your customer faces financial troubles he is unlikely to tell his suppliers about it. At the same time, it can be a huge relief for the customer if he knows that his supplier is willing to listen to him and think about ways to resolve the problem. Especially when financial problems are temporary, it can help both the customer and the supplier to openly discuss the matter, so you can both find practical and realistic solutions. Also, don't forget to inform the sales department, so that they know what going on as well. In both cases it is important to monitor the customer closely over the next few months and find a way to improve their payment behaviour.

EXCUSE #5

Customer: '*The payment has not been authorised, because the person responsible for approving invoices (departmental manager, procurement manager or general manager) is not available/out of the office.*'

Jenkins: '*I thought that you were responsible for all payment processes? Who needs to authorise this invoice and when will they be back?*' [wait for a reply] '*Does this mean that future payments will be delayed?*' [wait for a reply] '*I am not very pleased about this. The invoices are well overdue, so we need (stronger: have to) to find a solution today. Can you contact your colleague who can authorise payments, I will call you at [time] to see where we go from here. Is that OK?*' [wait for a reply]

Explanation

Hiding behind decision makers or procedures is something you will find in all kinds of organisations, especially within larger ones. Just when you need person X, he is not there or in a meeting. Large companies often work with so called payment procedures as a part of the procurement process. The invoice may be authorised, but when payment isn't, you still won't get your money. In practice it is very tough, if not impossible, to bypass these procedures. The best thing you can do is to build a good relationship with your contact in the accounts payable department. It will probably not change the authorisation procedure, but you may get a higher priority on the list of suppliers. It depends on the commercial and strategic importance of a customer as to what measures and adjustments of collections strategies you need to consider when this problem occurs often.

HINT /TIP 1

Sometimes it can be very hard to get hold of someone by phone to talk about outstanding invoices. In these situations it may help to let a colleague from sales or account management call the customer and ask for the same person. Customers with liquidity problems often don't like to talk about it. However, business does go on, so when your customers depend on deliveries for their own business to continue, they will still want to talk to people from sales. Once your sales or account manager has your contact on the line, he can easily put them through to credit management. Therefore a good relationship between sales and credit management is essential, so you can team up if required.

HINT /TIP 2

If you suspect that you are being fobbed off, because your contact is hard to get on the phone, then you may have to try alternative methods. Maybe the secretary is blocking you from talking to the managing director. In this situation it is important to stay in close control and get the secretary 'involved' in your goal. A very simple but effective method is asking direct questions, such as: 'When did you see or talk to Mr. X' or 'Did you pass on my message to Mr. X.? What did he say?' or 'Why did Mr. X. not call me?' By asking these types of questions it will become more difficult for the secretary to maintain her role of protecting her boss. Remember to stay friendly and asking the right questions can be a very effective way to get to where you want to be; in this scenario you want to talk to the managing director.

ATTENTION! Regarding payment issues, liquidity or cash flow problems, be aware that you **do not** discuss these with anyone other than your accounts payable contact at the customer. Payment problems can sometimes be very sensitive and if the boss is your contact, he will probably not appreciate it if you discuss the company's financial problems with one of his employees. So always be discrete when you talk about late payments or overdue invoices.

EXCUSE #6

Customer: '*We never received the goods!*'

Jenkins: '*I will immediately check with despatch, one moment please.*' [call despatch and ask if they can confirm the delivery and can send a copy of a signed delivery note]. '*If you didn't receive the goods, did your receive the invoice?*' [If the answer is yes.] '*Why didn't you contact us earlier, as I assume that you needed the goods you ordered?*' [wait for a reply] (meanwhile you have received a copy of the signed delivery note from the despatch department). '*I just received a signed copy of the delivery note, which proves that you have received and signed for the goods. I will email a copy of the delivery note to you now, so you can have a look at it and check internally. I will give you a call in an hour, so we can discuss payment of the outstanding amount?*' [wait for a reply]

Explanation

Every new customer should receive a copy of your terms and conditions. In these terms there is usually a section about non delivery or disputes and how to deal with them. This should include a time period in which claims for non or short delivery should be notified to the supplier. So a customer claiming that they have not received the goods, while having received the invoice, is actually breaking the terms and conditions. It may also indicate poor administration and handling of incoming goods at your customer. If this excuse is used often by the same customer, then it is advisable to monitor the customer more closely with regard to confirmation of receipt of goods.

It may be worth asking your despatch department to call them after the next few deliveries to confirm with them that the correct quantity and type of goods have been received.

HINT

When the goods arrive at the customer a delivery note needs to be signed, but also make sure that the name of the recipient is clearly readable (preferably get them to print their name underneath the signature). In practice and in particular when the driver is in a hurry the (electronic) delivery note often only has a (digital) signature but does not mention a name. When a delivery is disputed, it can save a lot of time if the name of the recipient is clear. Instruct your drivers or give clear instructions to your external logistics partner.

EXCUSE #7

Customer: *'My customer has not paid me yet.'*

Jenkins: *'I am sorry to hear that, but does that mean that you can't pay any invoices anymore?'* [wait for a reply]? *'Of course it is frustrating that your customer hasn't paid you, but I am afraid that this is no excuse not to pay us. Can you make a payment today?'* [wait for a reply] *'When do you expect your customer to pay you?'* [wait for a reply]. [Alternative 1]: *'We have to pay our suppliers and employees on time, so it is important that our customers pay us on time.'* [Alternative 2, if nothing else works] *'OK, as soon as you receive payment from your customer, which you are expecting on* [date expected payment], *can we agree that you will immediately pay the outstanding invoice(s).'* [wait for confirmation].

Explanation

This excuse is not only a poor one, but from a customer's point of view it is not a very smart one either. Often this excuse is an indication that your customer is experiencing liquidity or cash flow problems. It may also say something about his credit management policy. However, if you have a good relationship with your customer you should be able to discuss the issue openly and work on a practical solution. If progress is a bit sluggish, you could always try to turn the situation around and ask the customer how he would feel or act if he was in your position (tip 24). By confronting the customer with his own excuse, he will see that it is ineffective and harms him more than it helps him.

When the customer tells you that he expects his customer to pay soon and then he will be able to pay you, and if the invoice is not seriously overdue, you may accept this. Accepting this kind of excuse should be an exception, so you don't give your customer the idea that he can get away with it every time, by establishing a precedent. When this kind of excuse is used frequently by the same customer, always check the creditworthiness of the customer and discuss this with sales.

EXCUSE #8

Customer: *'The invoice was incorrect and I am still waiting for a credit note.'*

Jenkins: *'What exactly is wrong with the invoice?'* [wait for a reply] In this case it seems that the wrong discount was applied: 5% when it should have been 15%. *'When did you realise this mistake?'* [wait for a reply] or *'Why didn't you let us know earlier, because now the invoice is now overdue?'* [wait for a reply] *'Surely you check the invoice on receipt? It is common practice to notify us of any problems with invoices within five working days, so maybe in future you could let us know as soon as possible. I will make sure that you receive a credit note and a correct invoice as soon as possible and check our systems to make sure that this does not happen again. I will let you know when the credit note and the new invoice are processed, so you can arrange immediate payment. Is that OK with you?'* [wait for a reply]

Explanation

Queries regarding incorrect invoices, deliveries or damaged goods should always take place within the timescale as stated in your terms and conditions. Since queries regarding incorrect invoices, prices or discounts, are frequently made after the invoice is due for payment it is important to pay extra attention to this category. In contrast, in the case of incorrect deliveries your customer will most likely call you the same day. Of course it can sometimes happen that the customer forgets to let you know. Always check if claims for incorrect deliveries are valid or not and conduct analysis afterwards. Ultimately any claims should be kept to a minimum, as they have a negative impact on the business process, costs, cash flow and the customer relationship. If claims are made frequently and after the invoice is due, it is a good idea to temporarily check new deliveries and invoices as soon as they have taken place. Also discuss the matter with sales and logistics.

EXCUSE #9

Customer: *'The order was cancelled.'*

Jenkins: *'I can't see any notification on our system. Who did you discuss this with and when?'* [wait for a reply]. *'Did you cancel the order by telephone or in writing?'* [wait for a reply]. [Where the customer informs you long after the delivery was made] *'Why didn't you call us as soon as you received the goods?'* [wait for a reply]. *'One moment please, I will contact our sales department.'* [following the conversation]. *'I just spoke with our sales department and they haven't received any cancellation of the order. Before I make a decision, I would like to discuss it with your account manager and then call you back to finalise the matter. Is that ok with you?'*

After talking to the account manager, it appears that he knows nothing about the cancellation either. The order was placed at the customer's office and signed by him. The account manager decides that this order should not be taken back. You call the customer back.

'I have talked to [name account manager], *and he confirmed that you placed and signed the order at your office. This means that the order and delivery is valid and that the invoice should*

be paid.' [wait for a reply]. In this case the customer accepts the position. *'Now that we have resolved the problem would you arrange payment of the outstanding invoice this week?'*

Explanation

It happens to all of us that we sometimes make a mistake or that the market suddenly changes and as a result we have to cancel an order. It can also happen that a supplier sometimes ships an order that was previously cancelled by the customer. No matter what the reason, the customer needs to communicate incorrectly delivered orders or the delivery of cancelled orders in a timely manner. A good customer relationship can be very helpful, but prerequisites are transparency, honesty and timely communication from both sides. If the customer just responds when the supplier calls him chasing an overdue invoice, then you could say the customer has acted negligently. The standard rule is that any shipped order that has not been queried within a couple of days of delivery, should be considered a normal fulfilled order that has to be paid for within the usual terms.

On the other hand, don't play hard ball unnecessarily when the customer has accidentally made a mistake. Especially in cases where cancellation of an order is a rare event, don't make too much fuss about it and simply give in to the customers' wishes. Being flexible and bearing the costs of picking up the goods often benefits the customer relationship and future sales. Always make sure that your customers know how to act when they need to cancel an order and also instruct your sales people, so they can inform the customer as well.

Also make sure that your business processes and procedures are robust and easy to understand, so you will avoid unnecessary mistakes. This is usually a joint effort between sales, logistics, finance, credit management, service and IT. By efficiently working together, you can save a lot of time and costs, which benefits both the supplier and the customer.

EXCUSE #10

Customer: *'My customer went bankrupt.'*

Jenkins: *'I am sorry to hear that. What does this mean for your organisation?'* [wait for a reply] *'How did this happen? Were you taken by surprise?'* [the answer will give you more of an insight into the quality of your customer's credit (risk) management] *'I understand it must be very inconvenient and difficult for you, but if you went bankrupt tomorrow, should I tell my suppliers that I can't pay them for the time being?'* [wait for a reply] *'Despite your current cash flow problems, it is important that we find a solution. When do you expect to be able to pay?'* [wait for a reply] *'Two months? That seems a bit of a long time to me. I would suggest a payment plan/schedule, where you will pay* [amount part payment] *for the next (number of) weeks.'* [optional] *'Until you have fully paid the outstanding amount we are happy to ship new orders against advance payment.'*

Explanation

If a client of your customer goes bankrupt this could have a temporary negative impact on your customer's liquidity. Although a bankruptcy cannot always be predicted, it may say something about the quality and consistency of your customer's credit management and the way they monitor the creditworthiness of their customers. If a bankruptcy seriously impacts your customers liquidity or capacity to pay, this is an indication that your customer's financial status and liquidity is not very strong and you need to be more alert with this customer or issue a new credit check. A bankruptcy is of course an unpleasant and sometimes costly experience, but with proper credit (risk) management in place you should not experience this too often and it should not significantly impact a company's capacity to pay. A customer who tells you that due to the bankruptcy of one of his customers he cannot pay you, actually reveals more about his financial status and creditworthiness than he may realise.

EXCUSE #11

Customer: '*The financial paperwork is at my accountant's office.*'

Jenkins: '*When will your accountant return the paperwork?*' [wait for a reply] '*In two weeks? Can I suggest that since the invoices are well overdue, I send you a copy of them by email, so you can arrange payment today? Is that alright with you?*' [wait for a reply]

Explanation

This excuse can't be used by the customer too often. After all, how many times a year do you visit your bookkeeper or accountant and leave all your paperwork? Using this excuse implies that your customer would also not be able to pay his other suppliers, which is quite unlikely. When used more frequently, it is often an indication of financial problems. The best way to deal with this excuse is to send the customer a copy of the invoice(s) and ask him to pay immediately. If the customer still refuses to cooperate, you can always tell the customer that slow payment may delay new deliveries or in the worst case put the customer on stop.

EXCUSE #12

Customer: '*The managing director is on holiday and he needs to approve the payment.*'

Jenkins: '*When will your MD return?*' [wait for a reply] '*And does this mean that you can't pay other suppliers as well?*' [wait for a reply] '*Unfortunately, since the outstanding invoices are seriously overdue, if you cannot arrange payment all shipments may be delayed.*' [this is a friendly way of saying that the customer is put on delivery hold/stop]. '*How can we resolve this problem?*'[wait for a reply]? If the customer doesn't want to cooperate, you can apply more pressure. '*I really don't want to put you on stop, but you leave me no choice unless you pay the overdue invoices. I hope you understand my position. If you can pay earlier, please give me a call. Otherwise I would suggest you make an urgent payment as soon as your MD has returned from his holiday.*' [wait for a reply] '*OK I will contact you on* [the date the MD returns], so we can resolve the matter.*'

Explanation

A managing director who 'suddenly' goes on holiday and doesn't leave clear instructions for his staff, or doesn't authorise one or two employees to make payments is, in fact, an example of poor management. It is not only bad to act like this, but it also leaves a bad impression about the mentality of their supplier (relationship) management. It is also bad for the employees, because they are not able to resolve financial matters if required. This is clearly not the way to do business and a chat with the managing director when he returns from holiday wouldn't hurt. In a good and productive customer relationship, it should be possible to say that you are not pleased with this kind of behaviour. Prevention is always best, so pay a bit more attention to your customers before the holiday season starts and make clear arrangements with your customers about payments during the holidays so you can avoid the situation described above.

Dealing with late payment excuses.

The schedule below may be helpful in showing how you can deal with excuses for late payment. With a lot of practice and listening to your customers and colleagues, you will automatically learn how to deal with almost any excuse in an effective and customer-friendly way.

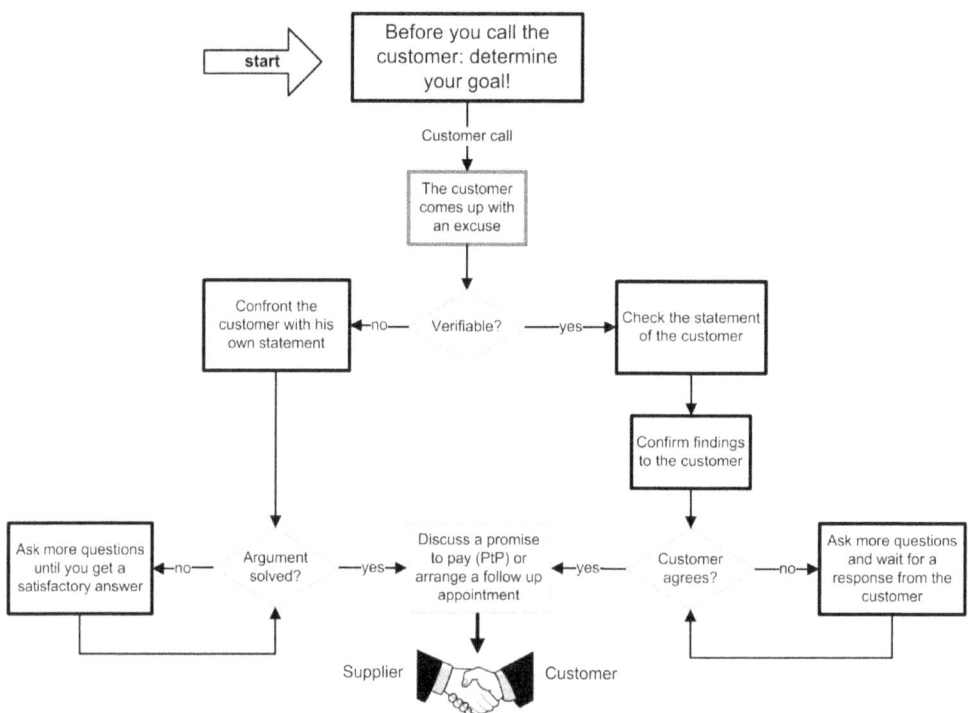

Figure 1: Flowchart dealing with excuses

The authors

Declan Flood

Declan Flood has worked in Credit Management all his life. He is recognised as *the* expert on all aspects of Credit Management in Ireland and beyond. With over twenty years' experience, any credit problem that you could encounter he has either the solution or knows the best person available to help you. He is recognised as a thought leader in Credit worldwide for his Total business approach to Credit. He believes that credit is not only about getting paid in full and on time, it is also about maintaining excellent customer relationships, finding a way to deliver every order and to streamline the business processes from Prospecting to Cash for maximum profit for every business. He can be contacted by email on declan@thecreditcoach.ie

Marcel Wiedenbrugge

Marcel Wiedenbrugge is managing director of WCMConsult. Marcel combines knowledge and experience in account management/sales, credit management, service management and related software solutions. In the past he worked for companies like Ricoh, Van Ommeren Ceteco, PCD Polymere and Yamaha Musical Instruments Europe.
Most of the time he worked in a B2B environment, but he is also quite familiar with retail. Marcel is an entrepreneur, speaker, writer, researcher, trainer and consultant. He develops, organizes and conducts workshops, trainings and seminars. He frequently writes articles and is the author of several books.

www.wcmconsult.com   marcel.wiedenbrugge@wcmconsult.com

Cliff Wynn

Cliff Wynn is managing director of RK Business Training Ltd. Cliff has both experience of working in the training, collections and tracing industry for many years. He has also worked with and for many of the leading professional bodies within the credit and collections industry, including the role of Head of Training for the Institute of Credit Management. He has built up a considerable knowledge of running a training business plus has 'hands on' experience of telephone and doorstep collections, compliance, consumer credit licence applications and tracing. During his career Cliff has worked with many large organisations on various training programmes in the collections area. Clients have included, Orange, Shell, Marston Group, Brighthouse, NPower, British Gas, Polycom BV, and the Finance and Leasing Association.

www.rkbusinesstraining.co.uk   cliff@rkbusinesstraining.co.uk

Notes

Notes

www.ingramcontent.com/pod-product-compliance
Lightning Source LLC
Chambersburg PA
CBHW071600170526
45166CB00004B/1739